Book of the Unknown Painter

Published by LOCATION-BKS 2026

For information on licensing, press inquiries, or discounts on bulk purchases for art schools: info@location-bks.com

Cover/interior design by Scott Nedrelow and Ruben Nusz

Logo design by Scott Nedrelow

Developmental and line editing by Tess Rankin

The Chicago Manual of Style (17th ed.)

www.location-bks.com

LOCATION-BKS
Submissions. Always. Welcome.

400 S. 4th Street
Suite 401 #1308
Minneapolis, MN 55415

Printed in Canada

Distributed by Itasca Books
210 Edge Place, Minneapolis, MN 55418

First Edition

ISBN: 979-8-9927572-0-0

Introduction

These collected aphorisms were recorded one summer while an unnamed artist lived in China. But they span a lifetime of reflection on painting, inspired by Greek philosophy, ancient artistic idioms, Tai Chi, and a range of other influences, both new and old. These insights—brief, meditative, expansive, and at times laden with wit—explore how an artist, or anyone seeking a creative outlet, might live in accordance with their work and the world.

At its core, the book explores a fundamental distinction: the telic versus the atelic. The former is destination-bound, emphasizing an endpoint; the latter describes actions without a defined conclusion, like listening to music. Throughout the book, the anonymous author, known only as The Painter, invokes the need to envision painting as an act rather than an object, emphasizing the verb over the noun. To be fully appreciated, painting, according to the author, must be performed rather than merely looked upon.

Like painting itself, this book has no fixed beginning or end. Chapters group the aphorisms for flow, but readers are free to enter and exit as they wish. Feedback and additions for future volumes are cordially invited.

LOCATION-BKS

Book of the Unknown Painter

Vielleicht sind wir hier, um zu sagen: Haus,
Brücke, Brunnen, Tor, Krug, Baum, Fenster—
höchstens: Säule, Turm.
Aber um sie zu sagen, muß man sie sehen.

Perhaps we are here in order to say: house,
bridge, fountain, gate, pitcher, fruit tree, window—
at most: column, tower.
But to speak these things, one must see them.

—Rainer Maria Rilke, *The Duino Elegies*

There is nothing more truly artistic than to love people.

—Vincent van Gogh

A Vision

If you stare at the world long enough, the urge to paint will come.

Painting rises into existence when summoned, like the sound of a struck bell.

Painting is like blinking. The hand and the brush are one—the strokes an unconscious reflex when needed, a controlled gesture when willed.

The language of painting transmits ideas, history, and culture in the guise of a charming heirloom.

A painting can hide many things, but never the intent of the painter.

Simplest advice for new painters: Paint daily, as if the world depended on it. Even though it doesn't. After a while, you won't be able to paint like this, so frenetically. But the habit will remain.

A painting often presents itself as a familiar form—this allows viewers to let their guards down. They don't have to question whether the object is art, only whether it has value to them.

You have to be willing to think and behave atypically when painting, ad extremum. I once knew a painter who decided to paint a landscape in their vast, country backyard. When they had finished, they realized that the work was imperfect—they had neglected to include one of the trees. So they went out to their shed, found an axe, and cut that tree down.

Being human is a negotiation: with yourself, with other humans, and with time. Painting, too, is a negotiation: between the hand and the eye, between the past and the present. Between a painter and a stranger.

Painting isn't about creating an object; the experience of looking at a work of art recalibrates the viewer's vision. And, of course, the painter's vision as well.

Why shouldn't a painting be like a yawn?

It would be absurd to think our aesthetics don't broadly reflect our culture. Still, sunny days are sunny days. Babies are beautiful. And then...there's springtime.

Pick a random person on the street and they could tell you what a painting is: "Anything covered with paint." A painter must discover the ineffable qualities that charge the material(s).

In painting, you can't say, "I will paint in this style." It won't work. The disingenuousness will be evident to anyone who sees the work. Style emerges from taking the long way, which, paradoxically, allows an artist to take liberties—shortcuts in executing their vision.

Don't be embarrassed if your style resembles someone else's when you start, especially if they are a conventionally admirable painter. But avoid the temptation to linger there; you'll often be praised for your work by those blind to your influences.

The etymology of painting can be summed up in three words: Decorate with color.

An artist must maintain a singular focus when painting, like shooting an arrow through the eye of a needle. The metaphor sounds impossible, until you do it. Artists are limited only by the breadth of their imaginations.

At times, in the studio, you don't have to use your hands. Often, looking, with intent, is enough.

Sometimes painting is like a key to a door, behind which is another door. Thus revealing the first door to be a facsimile.

One's character is content (CON-tent). That is to say, what an artist paints is shaped by who they are.

A painting's justification often becomes its subject.

"Why is this painting even here?" I've often asked myself. Does it really belong in this world? We'd never question a person's right to exist in such a way. But a painting must stake a claim for being. It must argue, on its own, without explanation, that it has a valid right to occupy space.

A painting is like a memory that works forward, not backward.

A critic once said, disparagingly, that a well-known writer's stories were a "technique in search of a subject." Honestly, as a painter, I think that sounds like a fantastic way to work.

If we are no more than our thoughts, then painting is physical thought. Us made manifest.

One day, I was home sick and unable to paint. In the morning, I saw a red cardinal in a green-leafed tree. Then, in the evening, on the way to the doctor, I saw a blue jay in a blue sky. The next day, I was able to paint.

When painting, you must maintain a contradiction in your mind—that of addition and subtraction. With each addition, something is subtracted. With each subtraction, something is added.

In painting, you create one world by destroying another. In the end a created world remains, ostensibly, until entropy repeats the process anew—all colors are bound to fade.

Attempting to paint the world accurately is like trying to paint pebbles through the rippling lens of a pool of water. Instead, be the water that distorts the vision.

The goal of the artist is to find the truest version of the self. The cause of the viewer is to use the artist's work as a guide to help them do the same.

I always wanted my paintings to be like butterflies: small, colorful, profound, timeless. The encounter brief but uplifting.

Our perceptions are entangled with our subjective experiences. When we try to paint the world, we imagine ourselves transcribing an objective reality laid out before our eyes. But really, we're documenting our affectations.

Gestalt theory says that we don't "see" the whole world with our vision. We see it selectively. But selective vision is vision. The two are inseparable. Painting, then, is an act of further selection. Great painting happens when an artist highlights aspects of vision that others overlook.

One morning in the studio, I closed my eyes and named every color I saw aloud. Then I spent the day mixing these colors, blinking and painting—mostly alizarin crimson and cadmium yellow, smudged onto a series of canvases. The paintings were uninspired. I learned the value of stillness. And the value of keeping one's eyes shut.

Painters are prisms.

Painting is old, older than our known religions and intertwined with the ancient burial practices of a hundred thousand years ago. Our ancestors would paint the bodies of the dead. Why? Painting has always been about continuity.

An artist's role is to say, "You are not alone." If the work is effective, the receiver thinks, I am not alone. Our internal lives are not only inside ourselves. Painting reveals this! Our minds have sisters.

Materials & Methods

There is joy in falling snow, just as in preparing to paint.

Once you have narrowed down the choice of materials, only the image matters. The idea you're communicating will seep through without your even thinking it. Many artists will "backdate" talking points they've fabricated once a work is finished—these are often lies.

Painting is a series of binary responses to materials, ones and zeroes, yeses and noes, which somehow ends in a soft "Maybe." Or perhaps: "This will do for now."

In painting, you create reality, and the converse is also true. The brush turns on itself. The self extends to the end of the bristles.

Even the best intentions should be left out of painting.

Painting is color in two dimensions that aspires to be in three.

Drama comes from placing a color beside its inverse. Harmony comes from placing a color beside its neighbor. The hammer and the nail of painting.

Colors are the Rosetta stone.

The arbitrary, too, has a place in painting. Welcome random, even bad, decisions like visits from family members. After a few days, send them home.

If you make an abstract painting with red, green, and blue, a viewer will see and recognize these colors. This is a form of realism. These colors are real—they can be named. I love De Stijl, but I wonder if a painting becomes even more abstract when the artist uses colors that resist definition.

Marble is marble, canvas is canvas. Pigment is pigment. Be mindful of the binder; it functions like the roots of the tree.

Painters waste pigments to save a moment.

Use the biggest brush possible: fifty strokes or fewer.

All painting aspires to the condition of sunlight.

Attach your brush to a long rod and try painting from a distance. Sometimes we just need to step back to see things clearly.

Be deliberate with your words. So too with the paintbrush.

If you try to hide how you made an object, you subtract the temporal element of discovery for the viewer.

When painting, don't forget to breathe. This is very important.

If in trouble, look at your painting and paint over each element that refuses to serve the whole.

The goal of still-life painting, most painting, is to create the effect of movement, demonstrating animistic forces at play in the inanimate. There are many ways to do this. Dark objects have light "afterimage" outlines, and the reverse is also true. You can paint these outlines, letting the natural shake of the hand personify the observation. When "long-looking" you'll notice the vibration of things. It all shimmers.

When painting something cold, use a blue ground. When painting something warm, a yellow ground. These colors will seep through once you paint over them. Every layer matters.

The ground of the painting is as important as the subsequent layers. A baker never frosts a turd.

All this talk about painting can be helpful, but there is something called the theory of the hammer: You won't know a thing about it until you actually grasp the handle and feel the hammer's weight in your hand.

At the end of a painting day, try mixing all of the colors of your palette into one muddy brown. Use it as a unifying color for the next day's painting. It may be a mess; it often is, but it may lead to something.

Cleaning is always better than painting. What I mean here is that cleaning can be a respite from the open-ended process of making art. It is like reverse entropy. And the process of sweeping the studio feels like wiping away the cobwebs from one's head.

Ha! A clean studio is like a clean kitchen floor—the children must be hungry.

When you're struggling, stretch one hundred canvases and prime them. Now you have no excuses.

In the wrong context, even the best paintings can look terrible. Sometimes, we as painters want to make things that feel severed from the world, like meteors. But this isn't possible. It's all the same substance. We're all the same substance.

More labor doesn't make a painting better any more than cooking a bird three times will make it more delicious.

Some artists like to say that art is less about what it reveals than about what it hides. This is both true and untrue. I realize this opinion equivocates. Subtext remains critical to art, but painters must never ignore the surface of things because for some viewers, that's all they see.

A painter without patience is no painter.

Just as teenagers carve their names into the trunks of trees, so too do artists make marks, signing that which cannot be owned with their egos.

It's always better to help someone than to paint. Especially children.

Just as a bonsai master would never over-prune a tree, for fear of killing it, a painter must also be careful: Each stroke, counterintuitively, is like the snip of the pruning shears.

Painting: pigments enlivened with empathy.

Even the most banal subjects—a small group of bottles—painted with an empathetic hand can be transcendent.

A good painting is like a stone hung on the wall: solid, heavy, interesting.

Paint over any painting that you wouldn't wrap up as a wedding gift.

In painting, there is no substitute for good habits. Those who paint every day improve. Our mothers were right: "Brush your teeth."

Like a man who refuses to sit on a bench in a beautiful park for fear of dirtying his new pants, a painter who fears making messes risks missing the moment.

Conceptual art can be dull because it often appears too controlled—there are no accidents. Without accidents, there are no surprises. No surprises, no drama. Accidents, I would argue, are the most critical part of painting. Accidents allow you to easily elicit a realm beyond the self.

There are times you'll find yourself going through the motions. Like making dinner every night. That's why exhibitions matter. They're like cooking for company.

Executing poor brushstrokes is like whipping a horse while riding. What do you hope to accomplish, and why do you need to get there so quickly?

"I think I've forgotten how to paint," I said aloud in the studio one morning. Then, I loaded up the palette and painted.

There is a vast immensity of possibility in a brushstroke: It can be foliage, a highlight on a milk jug, or a mustache. It can come forward or recede in an illusory fashion. It can be color and/or a line. It can be a fingerprint or a part of a gestalt. Or it can be wholly itself, a pigmented touch from an artist's hand.

I bought a fancy Chinese paintbrush with a curved bamboo handle. It was such a beautiful handle. I almost didn't want to use it. When I finally tried it, the bristles turned out to be poor. Now, it hangs as decoration. Soon, I'll throw it away.

Imagine a tree that grows next to a rock wall. When the wind blows through its branches, one rough-tipped branch scratches at the stone, carving it over time. Who really carved the stone? The wind or the tree?

Teachers, Students & Influences

A Christian monk once brought his student outside.
"Insult this stone," he said.
The student did so.
"Did the stone answer back?"
"No," said the student.
"Painters should be like the stone. Take offense at nothing."

When visiting another artist's studio, remember that nothing is emptier than a discovery unearned.

What would you be embarrassed to paint? Paint that.

Don't be worried about copying a dead painter's strokes. An artist must learn to speak a thousand languages before inventing a new one.

Tradition, when adhered to strictly, is a prison of the spirit. But without tradition we are like snakes without bones, flowers without stems.

Imagine all of the world's paintings tossed into a bonfire. Which would you try to save? Not for the culture but for yourself. These are your teachers.

You don't need to know the names of every tree to enjoy a walk in the woods. The same is true in the museum.

Visiting a museum is like visiting a graveyard. No need to stop at every marker, only those you love.

Respect those who know more than you, of course. But beware of those who wield their "expertise" to diminish your experience.

There is no singular way to interpret a painting. Those who think otherwise would have you cut out your own eyeballs to see with theirs.

Using historical knowledge of painting to intimidate invalidates one's perspective. Knowing more about an apple doesn't change its sweetness.

Young painters, just because your teachers' paintings lack merit doesn't mean their lessons do. Great teachers aren't always great painters. Of course, the reverse also holds true.

You won't find what you're searching for in those museum salons, in those galleries, in the halls of your teachers. Only painting can teach you to paint.

Young painters, you will need at least two years to learn to draw, two years to learn to move the brush, and two years to learn to mix color—it takes a lifetime to master the latter.

I once heard an artist say, "When color fails." Color isn't a student. Color is. Only artists fail—they fail when they neglect to present color with reverence.

When you first start painting, work in black and white. The human eye sees value (light and dark) hierarchically over color. Wittgenstein, in Remarks on Colour, talks about a blond boy in a black-and-white photograph, illustrating how perception is based on context. We see the boy's hair as blond even though the image is black and white. Reminders like these point to the sophistication of the human eye and the power of grisaille.

Often, those who know the least about painting give the best advice. You don't have to take it literally.

The greatest painters are the greatest teachers—not with their words, but through their works.

Painting fulfills desires many of us didn't know we had—one of which is the urge to create the world, not merely experience it.

Being an artist isn't like being a lawyer or a doctor. It's not an official career. An artist shouldn't seek degrees. Nobody cares where Frida Kahlo studied or how wealthy Cézanne's family was. Painting, only painting.

Trust a few artists whose work you respect. Fewer than fingers on the hand.

Young painter, I haven't seen your paintings, but I know your desires. I recognize them because I once shared them. I know your colors are misguided. You rush where you should wait; you linger where you should move like a breeze.

Most young painters suffer from one problem: color. Their selections are too facile. Unearned. Shallow. Lacking depth. Arbitrary.

How do you improve the color relationships in your paintings? Simple. Copy the greats until you understand color relationships on an unconscious level. Then destroy or paint over all the copies.

In some ways color relationships in painting are like narrative cinema. Figure out who the leads are and then build around them with supporting actors.

Visiting some advanced students, I realized that the advice I often gave was consistent with what I tell all beginners: Keep painting.

A young business student once asked me about my profession. I said, "I'm a painter." He said, "Wow, so that's your job?" I said, "No, painters don't have jobs. That's why we paint."

Always assume that your audience is smarter than you. Because they are, and I don't just mean collectively.

Sometimes art schools can be problematic because they overemphasize criticality and underemphasize generosity. It's okay to skip class and look at the world. Most importantly, stay curious. Paint.

Never trust an artist who hands you a business card. But don't hesitate to make connections with anyone, whether they might be supportive of your work or not. Most painters work alone, but you can't exhibit that way, and you can't grow that way. Works of art are tools to help dissolve the "illusion of separateness."

If possible, avoid conversations about art with more than one person at a time. Groups in critique settings are better at tearing things down than building them up.

Sometimes I find myself in such desperate need for insight that I'm willing to criticize anything.

But I've learned to hesitate in criticizing the young. Why? They invariably have the last word.

The Taoist approach to painting is simple: to paint without painting.

Imagine two dogs in a house, each with its own bowl. One dog sometimes eats from the other dog's bowl if its food is poured first. The second dog then must eat from the first dog's bowl. Competition between painters is no different.

Trade painted idols and aspirations for daily practice. You'll be surprised how liberating painting can be when the emphasis is less on the wall and more on the hand.

And yet, the names of the painters we recognize—Van Gogh, Jacob Lawrence, O'Keeffe—and their best-known paintings represent an accomplishment, to be sure. These painters have managed to transform their consciousnesses into objects. Their names are synonymous with their works: They have become paintings themselves.

Be careful with critiques. Gentle conversation is beneficial, and often a necessary part of the process, but critiques can push one down a path toward disingenuousness, which is the enemy of art.

A student asked her teacher why people were not responding to her work. "The problem," said the student, "is that their reactions were neither positive nor negative, but rather ambivalent." The teacher replied, "Well, your colors need work, but more importantly, you're missing conviction. Better to be hated for something you believe in than loved for something you don't."

Sit. Stand. When painting, it doesn't matter. Each affects the style differently. Lucian Freud's style changed when he stopped sitting and started standing to make paintings. I like both the early and late pictures. Funny, I had a teacher who told me: "Always paint with your shoulder." Great advice, so long as you're not painting miniatures.

A young painter was walking with an old painter. They walked in silence for a long time.

Painters are like empty paper cups, eager to fill up with anything that will keep the wind from blowing them over.

The best advice I ever received was not from a professor but from an acupuncturist. As he was about to stick me with needles, he gently pushed on my hip to calm my body, and as my body relaxed, he said, "Don't worry."

What we love about painting is its humaneness, its humanity. Honor your teachers like you would your parents. Call your mother.

One winter, a teacher was instructing a student who kept overworking her paintings. The student didn't know when to stop painting, when a painting was finished. The teacher asked her to go outside, walk into the woods amid the newly fallen snow, shape a ball in her hands, and bring it indoors. The student did so. The teacher instructed the student to place the snowball in a bowl and said, "Start on a new painting. Finish when the snow has melted."

Sometimes, I'll hear my name called when I'm sleeping. I wake up, and no one is there. I'm not sure how this relates to painting, but I will say that teachers are there to help you. Then they're gone, and you're on your own. But they're never really gone.

Mind & Ego

To paint well, the mind must fast.

Ideas can weigh a painting down, like rain on the petals of a flower.

We do not know how to fall asleep, yet we all do it daily. Painting is just like this.

I'm trying to be more like a spider, waiting in my web, letting things happen.

If there isn't doubt in your mind, even fear, before painting, you probably don't know painting.

If the brush fails, use your hands. If the hand fails, use your feet. If none of it works, your mind is wrong.

In Buddhism, the mind is said to be treacherous. A brush, like a sword, can be used to kill the mind.

I find that if I do not maintain a singular focus on painting, if I allow other, critical voices into my head, then the work suffers. I have to remind myself that color is the mantra.

Painters attempt to illuminate the darkness, to see the impossible darkness. I don't know how else to describe this but through sound. Imagine a lone wolf, a long distance away, howling into the void.

Painting is nature: Ants build mounds. Humans decorate walls with ideas.

What we love about painting is not only the aesthetics but also an artist's ability to solve problems, mostly formally—their capacity to look at dead ends and see nothing but possibilities.

Painters are beloved because, like scientists, they bring order to chaos. But unlike scientists, painters are free to dwell in disorder.

The worst artists have no teeth. They blindly gum their surroundings, seeking approval for discoveries the rest of us can plainly see.

Artists are all narcissists, painters most of all. If you think otherwise, paint over each day's work with the next day's and tell no one what you do in the shadows.

Painting is the residue of ego.

The great contradiction: Artists must reconcile the ego of individualism, which generally gives an art object preciousness, with the desire to connect with the universal.

Art lies between ego and cliché. Too much of the individual and people can't relate. Too much of the universal and viewers will think they've seen the work before.

Portrait painters paint the guts, not the face.

It's better to remember paintings than the names of painters.

You must know the work of five painters unknown to other painters. Otherwise, your work will probably look familiar to everyone—unless you truly know how to capitalize on your accidents.

If you think you can hide yourself in a painting, you're wrong. Painting reveals who you are. If your paintings are smart, that's you! If they are joyful, that's you! If they are boring, that's you too. Don't let this bother you. There's plenty of room for boring paintings in the houses of boring people.

You don't owe painting anything. Painting doesn't owe you anything. There are no debts. But a gift scorned is a shame.

A painter once lived in the mountains alone. She painted every day except Sunday, when she hiked into town to sell her work. One day, a man asked her why she painted. "You've seen the world," she said. "You've seen all the sadness by now." He nodded and walked away.

To enjoy painting, one must set aside cynicism, like removing your shoes when entering someone's home.

The devil's voice inside—the internal critic—is (unfortunately) always right and (fortunately) always wrong.

Looking at art about art is like watching a snake eat its own tail.

Each painting is only a fragment of the artist's larger understanding. The learning is a work unto itself; the painting, a footnote.

All an artist is ever looking for is an external confirmation of their internal world.

Just as we use religion and mythology to soften the discomfort of existence, so too can we use painting. Quiet acts calm a noisy mind.

I still fall prey to the feeling that if I could just make a work of enduring art, I would experience a sense of contentedness. But nothing endures. There is comfort to be found in this. And freedom.

We are able to empathize with objects when an artist can anthropomorphize more than merely dogs and cats, but grapes and strawberries. To see the love in a bunch of asparagus (Manet) or a carcass of beef (Rembrandt) in all its sadness—that is beauty, if we can still use such a word.

But remember, empathy for objects is not the goal. It is only a tool to cultivate affection for humanity, the earth, and the self.

To open the aesthetic mind, look externally. All other minds require introspection.

Most of us painters are vain. As we age, we compensate with our brushes for what we lose on our faces.

Painters are often the people who open their mouths, and their words misbehave.

Artists are insecure. If they weren't, they wouldn't try so damn hard to differentiate themselves from others by acting like fools.

I've always thought gargantuan paintings could only be made by painters with gargantuan egos. Maybe I'm wrong.

In painting, individual talent is overrepresented, held up as the ideal. I don't want to dissuade anyone from acknowledging greatness, but I do wonder if an emphasis on the collective language of painting would open up the medium to more people.

Painters attempt to move people in some way, emotionally, I suppose. They fail when the painter's vanity supersedes their sincerity.

To fathom another's heart and mind, that is empathy. It's also an apt description of looking at paintings.

I don't know how else to say this, but be natural. A river both dictates its course and follows the course laid out for it.

People live their lives as strangers. All of us strangers. Nearly none will know my paintings or yours. Painting is a futile gesture. Painters are like obsessives who count each one of their breaths.

Art is like a plant growing inside of the ear. We listen but cannot hear. We look, but our eyes cannot see. We press our fingers in but feel nothing. The growth happens, nonetheless. Search inside, and you will sense it. Artists turn their heads inside out.

Dostoevsky said that the more intelligent you are the more you suffer. I'm reminded of that old phrase, "Dumb as a painter." What do I mean by this? The mindlessness of painting can mollify suffering.

Creativity is no mystic secret. It is the ability to welcome mistakes and serendipity as if they were intentions, refract them so they appear premeditated, and then justify the whole process as if it were guided by insight.

Artists are searchers. They spend most of their lives looking for something. Painting, on a micro level, embodies the life of the artist: The artist searches for something new, finishes or abandons a painting, and discovers something else, only to abandon that in search of something else. When the artist no longer searches, they will no longer need painting.

Painting in Time

Time—you can't go back. But you can paint back.

Painting resurrects the present, folding each moment upon itself.

If you are not attempting to manipulate time and space, why paint?

When presenting how you, the painter, have created something from nothing, it is best to show how you got there. The path is where the story resides. An ending without a story is just an ending.

If you feel guilty or anxious wasting time, then go punch a clock.

Someone once said that the warp and weft of the canvas provided the first structure that led to modern painting, a natural grid. But I feel like the first structure was a rectangular shape—a coffin. How can you fit life into a box? Kill nature? No. Let things take their course.

I've made paintings for years. Too many to count. They're not great, but they're getting better. That's enough. If you can't be as good as the painters you admire, just be better than yesterday.

But some days, it's better not to paint. Especially when you don't feel like it. Don't worry. Your paintings aren't going anywhere. When you return, they'll either be better or worse than you remember. If they are better, then you were too hard on yourself. If worse, you'll quickly discover why.

To avoid anxiety, paint every day. The hand is wiser than the head.

A painter has six senses: touch, taste, smell, hearing, sight, and, most importantly, patience.

Spend a whole day with a blank canvas and do nothing. The next day, painting should be easier.

I know I am a minor artist, on par with a hobbyist. I haven't painted any big pictures, great pictures. This used to sadden me. I had grand ambitions. Thankfully, my mindset has changed. The only thing that matters now is the language. But, like most elder painters, I feel I have so much to teach those starting out, but too little time. That is the common denominator of every painter: "Too little time."

Without reverence for the past, one cannot expect reverence for the present.

You make a painting in the present. The future determines if it is art.

A great painting is like having nostalgia for a place you've never been to, in a time that never was.

Maybe there are no more great painters. Perhaps the greatest painters have all died, have gone extinct. I think this is for the best. It opens up the language to more people. We don't need to be echoed names. We simply need to learn the language and share it with others.

Most mediocre painters insert their own narratives into predetermined forms defined by the past.

Death is the ultimate abstraction. Great painters don't fear death. They fear not painting.

According to Taoist texts, life that gives life is endless. Color that creates color is also endless. Red never dies.

A painter's dream: to die, paint the other side, return, and show the world there is nothing to fear.

Is this the last painting you will paint? It might be.

Don't confuse painting with religion. Painting can't save you. It only offers a way to consider time and assuage ennui.

One of the biggest differences between the worldviews of the East and the West is in their respective concepts of time. Most in the West see time as linear; most in the East see time as cyclical. How does this apply to painting? I certainly am in no position to determine if time is linear or cyclical, but painting seems to be both.

Painting is as old as religion. It has always been beloved by little children, who use it to communicate with a deeply felt directness. On the day children refuse to paint, only then will painting be dead.

Sport is living myth. Painting is history enlivened by the hand.

Some say painting evolved from mapmaking. Untrue: Painting existed long before maps, but the premise sounds like it makes sense. Even today, paintings are the maps of human consciousness.

Don't feel as if you are planting a tree when you paint. The roots of painting already run deep.

Between humbleness and arrogance lies the artist, who, even when they've perfected their craft, must still prostrate themselves before the past.

The best time to be a painter is now. The sweetest-smelling flowers aren't found flattened and folded in books.

To imagine painting as anything but ephemera is like a kid believing the summer will never end.

Spiders in the studio are good luck! They are painters from the past who've returned to witness the artists of the future.

Throughout history, the economic powers have always determined painterly popularity. Some might say, "Great painters aren't born. They're bought."

Painting is a form of clinging, an attempt to crystallize time. Trying to save a moment this way is like locking a child in a closet and praying they never grow up.

We cling to painting because life is fleeting, and painting possesses the illusion of longevity. If time is the ocean, we live like untrained swimmers—grasping at anything to keep us afloat in an attempt to deny our inevitable irrelevance.

When you are young, your eyes will deceive you, so you cannot trust them. When you are middle-aged and have seen the world's paintings, if you can't trust your own eyes, then what can you trust? When you are old, your eyes will deceive you once more, yet you will trust them.

Sit. Observe. Paint. Then, over time, stop painting. Stop observing. Stop sitting.

Freedom, Discipline & Doubt

Certainty is the purview of morticians, not artists.

I am unsure about everything I'm saying, but I am saying it anyway. The same logic applies to painting.

Sunday painters are great painters. They paint for themselves, not posterity.

These hobby painters, Sunday painters, paint on their day of rest. Contemporary painters should learn this balance and treat every day like Sunday—rigor with the ease of leisure.

Painting is no place for heroes.

Did you ever hear a friend say, "I have an idea! Let's throw a party tonight!" That's how each decision in your painting should feel.

Painting demands discipline and a lack of discipline. Freedom and rigidity. Talent and naivete. Certainty and doubt.

Maybe everything I know about painting is wrong. But I'm trying to make a "good wrong."

Painters are like monks. They share a devotion to something greater than themselves. The higher state of consciousness manifests in the practice, not the self. Why else would you have an exhibition except to share your insights?

The opposite of a painting is a fence.

Painters interrogate with their eyes, and their minds follow. This inevitably leads to questioning the self and life, if it's all worth it. It is. When I'm feeling down, I stretch more canvases.

More and more, I believe that what we love about certain paintings is the personalities behind them. I don't mean that we need to know the artist's life story. Rather, who they are, their thoughtfulness and discipline, their aches and affections are all embedded in the painting.

Some painters are so consumed by paranoia they won't let anyone visit their studios, afraid of others stealing their ideas. But one can't live fully while imagining enemies in every bush.

Genius is a word invented by those in power to dissuade others from hard work.

One day, a wild tiger found its way into a zoo and lay down outside the bars of a caged tiger. The caged tiger said, “Have you come to admire my comfortable life? Humans serve me my meals. I can sit here all day with the freedom to think my thoughts.” The wild tiger replied, “Our minds are only as free as our bodies.” The caged tiger said, “But you’ve no time to think. You have to spend all your time hunting and avoiding capture.” The wild tiger replied, “If I had all the time in the world to think, I would think only of hunting.”

Art allows the individual to break free from the bondage of the body to extend one’s consciousness out into the world—birdsong to receptive ears.

Just as prisoners mark each day with a scratch on the cell wall, so too do artists mark time. The difference is that the prisoner’s marks will never free them.

Sometimes, it feels like museums are prisons for objects made to personify freedom.

To make a painting with thirty strokes demands much more ingenuity than making one with three hundred, but a painting with no strokes, not even painting, that would be liberating.

Artists are birds; critics are worms. The worms will always envy the birds for their freedom.

Every interpretation of your work is a misunderstanding.

Do not stop painting if criticized or ignored. That would be like starving oneself for fear of choking.

Painting has a lot to do with insomnia. When the mind is restless, you toss and turn, rolling over onto your belly, your back, your side. But when you clear your mind and breathe, sleep quiets the noise. So too with painting. It situates you in yourself and silences all sounds.

Being a painter is like rock climbing without a rope, in the sense that when you have a regular job, such as building houses or picking up garbage or cooking food, you have a utility to hold on to psychologically, a rope, so to speak. You can be reassured knowing you are doing something useful. With painting, your utility will always be in question.

I'm averse to all forms of fundamentalism. Painters cannot be fundamentalists, in religion, politics, or other areas. They must be nimble and free, moving about like hummingbirds, unattached to ideas.

There are two types of artists: didactics and romantics. Didactics tell you something you know. Romantics tell you something you don't, and in a sexy way.

You walk along a path in the woods and find a beautiful stone. You hold it in your palms, admire its speckled surface, its color. You put it in your pocket and continue walking. Later, you discover another small stone. You roll this one between your fingers, enjoying its smoothness, its shape. You put this one in your other pocket. Farther along, you spot a third stone. You empty your pockets and continue walking.

When I can't paint, the reason often lies in ruminating on false failure, that is, failing to live up to exaggerated expectations. When those thoughts occur, just moving the brush helps.

Even to make a poor painting requires an open mind. A mediocre painting requires discipline and hard work. A great painting requires all these things and a willingness to fail and fail and fail.

Some days, you can make a painting. Some days, you can't even make the bed. Both are okay.

When in doubt, paint flowers.

A Day in the Life

Each day, I aim to unburden myself of things to do.

A young boy asked me once, "Did you draw yourself today?" I said, "I draw myself every day."

As children grow, so does their sense of self. Most adults believe their selves are resolved. Artists know otherwise—this is the way in which they are most like children.

As a painter, let empathy be your guide rather than aesthetics.

One has to be so bored in the studio that the only thing to do is paint.

If you get creatively stuck at the studio or at home, sit in your chair and wait. Look out the window. Watch the wind. Sometimes I feel the need to change my rhythm. To adapt to a different pace, a slower pace, like watching paint dry.

Painters should not concern themselves with being artists. Artists are interested in "the newest thing." Painters turn the stone around.

There is no path to becoming an artist that doesn't involve disappointing one's parents.

Art stands in for the unfamiliar. To make compelling work, you must familiarize yourself with as much of the world as possible. This means traveling, if you can, and looking at books and any painting you can get your eyes on. Stay hungry. Practice painting daily, with myriad techniques, new and old.

When traveling the world, if you don't know the language, that's fine. The language of painting can be understood by all painters. We see how the hand once moved.

There was a great painter who would make sculptures when he couldn't paint. Some painters write when they can't paint. If you think of painting alone, you'll only paint paintings. Even great painters have hobbies.

When painting, breathe naturally.

Breathing out is as vital as breathing in. We often consume breath like food. But breathing is not eating: The "out" balances the "in" and vice versa. When in doubt, breathe out.

Just breathe naturally.

I don't think I will paint today. What will the mice do with the cat away?

Too sick to paint, I draw. Too sick to draw, I write. Too sick to write, I read. Too sick to read, I watch the wind in the trees. Sometimes though, sleep is the only remedy.

Don't think, "Someday, I'll paint the perfect painting." Embrace the fortune of each day.

The most useful trait an artist can have is resiliency. This is true for life in general, I suppose.

Young painters, don't concern yourself with how to paint or even what to paint. Learn how to be in the world. How does one do that? I don't know, be generous.

On some painting days, I'll make a quick one. Then I'll try to repeat it, but what happens next is a sort of manufactured spontaneity—an affectation of a painting. A disingenuous failure.

A day without painting is like a summer day spent indoors.

An artist's studio is like a spiderweb—anything that enters sticks. Be wary of letting in those who do not care for spiders. They are snakes.

If you're looking for riches or accolades, don't bother painting. You'll find nothing more than the satisfaction of making a picture, which should be enough.

I've stepped away from painting for a bit to write this text. Maybe I should quit. There are times it seems pointless. So does everything. But if there's a better way to spend one's day than painting, I haven't found it.

When second-guessing yourself, just paint. The act forces your mind to abandon its ruminating. It transforms the mind into movement, into color, into image. This echo of consciousness can then be examined and enjoyed. What's the point of that? I don't know. But it's enough to keep me coming back.

I was playing cards with my niece and nephew. My eight-year-old niece would sing when she won and cry when she lost. I explained to her that each hand contained joy and suffering for someone. Why are you so special that you alone should experience joy while everyone else suffers? The sooner an artist realizes that they are not unique, the better. Only then can they focus on the task at hand: improving.

When has an artist ever been understood?

To say an artist is understood is like saying we understand rocks.

An artist must not be attached to being understood. Painters are only understood by dead painters.

If you have dark thoughts—and painters often do—rise early—retreat in the evening. Usually the light's better when the sun's up anyway. What am I saying. All light is good light.

Good wine. Poor wine. It makes no difference to the painting.

Sit back. The painting isn't going anywhere. Keep working until it does.

Take your favorite book. Cut it in half. Read the first half. Bury the second. That is what each day of painting is like. You can never read the second half, ever. That's why you keep painting, to continue the story.

Two painters were talking. One said, "I don't work on Sundays. I rest." "Oh, that's good," said the other painter. "You still paint, though, right?"

How a painter differs from a housepainter: One trades pigment for money, the other, pigment for the prospect of posterity. And sometimes, money.

Painting is a sad, solitary act wherein the artist asks questions of the air and answers with color.

My studio practice involves telling a joke and trying to repeat the joke in different ways to surprise myself, to make myself laugh, as if for the first time.

Painting

I've found something!
No, I've seen that.
I've found something!
No, I've seen that.
I've found something!

Brush. Canvas. Paint. What more do you need?

Diary entry 2/12/17

I painted today. Good day.

The Art of Looking

Some painters imagine that viewers will invest an amount of time into their paintings commensurate with the labor involved in making them. These painters champion "long-looking." I'm more pragmatic. Paintings are mosquitoes. The point is to draw blood.

Painting happens when the universe becomes conscious of itself, trying to observe its own existence. When we see and enjoy another artist's work, we don't see only ourselves, our humanity, we see, for lack of a better way to say it, an awareness of being.

I heard somewhere that everyone is watching, but no one is looking, because they're only watching themselves. A painting must be more compelling than the viewer's own reflection.

Look at the picture on Tuesday, then Wednesday, then Thursday, then Friday. Wait a week, look at it again, leave it alone. Keep looking. Don't destroy it if it keeps changing.

Pay attention to the little moving animals and watch them scurry. They are brushes, the earth their canvas.

Go for a walk. Find a turtle shell. Hold it up to your painting. If your painting is more interesting, it is done. Return the shell.

You must be able to reject what other painters would accept. This is taste.

To build upon La Rochefoucauld, neither a painting nor the sun nor death can be looked at steadily.

When an artist says that color can create light in painting, I think they've got it wrong. Color is light. Light is color. They arrive together like twins born side by side, pulling each other into the world.

There is no such thing as unnatural light. Is an anthill, because it is created by ants, not natural?

I like to keep the following proverb in mind when painting: "You say one thing. She understands three." We're not as smart as we think, and you won't fool anyone if your paintings lack intellect and effort.

A painting exhibition is like a funeral. But everyone shows up thinking it's a birthday party.

Works of art are made in caves that no one enters and displayed in plazas for all to see.

The concept of "local color" is meaningless. It assumes an objective color exists. But perception alters everything. Paintings show us how an artist sees, *and* how we see.

Better for a painting to be good than popular. Paintings aren't politicians.

At a certain age you'll realize that the simplest things are the hardest to paint: a leaf quivering in the wind, a speck of dust floating in a golden ray of sunlight, love.

It is possible that those who dislike your work lack the ability to perceive it. Possible, but highly unlikely.

The residual effects of artists connect the inanimate (creating from oblivion) to the animate (the artist) to the inanimate (the art object) and back to the animate (human perception).

Some painters have tried to abandon civilization in search of "purity." There exists only illusion and suffering. We can't escape these things. It's the artist's job to provide the vision for utopia.

Painting creates the illusion of certainty—creating something from nothing—in an uncertain world—where we move from being something to nothing.

Never trust anyone's opinion of a painting unless you've seen it yourself. This seems obvious but is often forgotten.

Painting: thinking in colors and writing in forms.

A painting should be like a handsome criminal.

Painters are like ghosts. They just want to be seen.

Painting—a definition:
A surface wherein a human being recreates their perceptions using colored pigments.

Another definition:
Stop talking, please.

When I enter a museum, I often think about how little I know. I let my eyes guide me like an intuitive live map. When I leave, I feel my eyes adjust to the space and the light outside. Somehow my eyes feel like they've been "tuned."

French Academic painter William-Adolphe Bouguereau describes painting as a process of looking and blinking and looking. This makes sense. Blinking will blur the image, making it easier to see forms as shapes. It also creates an aftereffect for colors and forms, giving dark shapes halos and light ones outlines.

Also, since humans see stereoscopically, by blinking individual eyes, each perspective flattens so that upon opening, you can see the discrepancy between the three- and two-dimensional qualities.

Painting, fundamentally, helps develop the skills of observation and transcription. Details of the world, for painters, become explicit: the glisten of moisture on a lower eyelid, the breadcrumb on the tie of a besuited diner, the blood pulsing through the veins between the knuckles on your mother's hand.

These skills of observation allow an individual to see more clearly. If one can see the world more clearly, one can see the suffering in the world. And if one sees suffering in the world and does nothing, then there is no hope for that individual. Put the brush down.

(Un)Finished Painting

A painting doesn't have to be perfect. It just has to be convincing.

Who are you, young painter? Do you think your name, your vision, your signature matter? All that matters is painting. Until you realize that, your paintings will be like toenail clippings.

Painting reveals how the hand once moved—like whispers of the dead.

Nonobjective painting remains popular largely because those in power generally prefer to support art that abolishes context. Context provides an awareness of privilege.

Mostly, galleries are places for people to play without hurting anyone.

I will always argue for the home as the best place for paintings. One day, I hope that great paintings will live on the walls of every house, but first, we must provide everyone with houses.

Paintings have value only in that they are irreplaceable, like dead pets.

A painting exhibition is a room full of mirrors. The danger comes when viewers look for themselves and find only you.

Yes, paintings are mirrors, and painters must be vampires, their reflections absent.

A painting should have a smell. Like a rose. Or a stew.

Painting resides where music hides.

Great paintings are like lights in the night, always attracting attention. Even if it is only us insects.

To waste what you have been taught and all that you have learned would be a shame.

Again, there are no great artists who lack compassion.

An old friend once said, "I'm a human being first, an artist second." That's pretty good.

An artist turns inward and like a surgeon, extracts what they find. A painting is the result of a successful operation.

Most painters paint until they die. Some paint until they've said, "Enough." I suspect the feeling is the same.

Artists' friends who give honest and unencumbered feedback help keep the dark side of doubt at bay. Some studio visitors don't even have to say anything. Just watch them look at the pictures. Study how long they linger on each one. Often, that's all the information you need.

That feeling—when you're walking in the park or the woods and you reach a point where no one is around, when loneliness washes over you, like you'll never see another human again—and then—the realization that you're surrounded by a family of trees and birds and other animals. You're not alone. You are never alone. That's what I'm trying to accomplish in painting.

Strong paintings can withstand criticism better than painters can. We're so sensitive. But paintings are tough: Insults bounce off them like balls tossed against a wall.

To attempt to resolve whether painting has any meaning would be like sucking a stone to satiate hunger.

Meaning in painting is owned by the passing glances of future eyes.

"Effortless effort" (wu wei) and painting seem obvious counterparts. But you can't achieve this state from the start of the practice by willing it. Only after years of labor does a painter reach the point where effort and ease align.

In youth, how can you know the wrinkles that will soon line your face? How can you anticipate the thinning of your hair and the arthritic pain in your fingers? A painting may be "finished," or rather abandoned, but its value can only be discovered with time.

Meaning or lack of meaning—these are equals when considered in the context of the broad expanse of time and history. We are so very insignificant, human beings. We are coughs between eternities, most of us at least. A few are songs.

Exhibitions are embarrassing. Not as embarrassing as dying, of course, but you must reveal your taste and what you do with your time and somehow convince other people that the way you see the world isn't completely ridiculous.

Painting need not be subversive. Perhaps it can't be anymore. But it can still assuage the isolation of existence.

When it comes to the great paintings, their conviction of vision overwhelms you, so much so that even stubborn heads nod in understanding.

Transcendence in painting is like the arrival of something you'd been waiting for, unaware that you'd been waiting at all.

When I think about the old painters, I sometimes experience envy. And then I think I'd rather not be any of those old names on the museum's walls. They're dead!!!

If you don't love every tree, every bush, every blade of grass, you cannot paint a landscape. If you don't love every feature, every wrinkle, every pore of the face, how can you try to paint a portrait? If you love only yourself, well, who would want to see that picture?

How do you know a painting is finished? In the pause between your efforts, hesitation takes hold; the desire for what you might gain fades with the fear of loss.

The Infinite Language

People will forgive almost anything in art. But not dishonesty.

Clever and erudite words don't improve a painting. Beware of painters with silver tongues and no pigment under their fingernails.

Painting manipulates light (color). Sometimes, I think it would be easier to control the wind.

Once, an artist painted a pristine landscape by a pond. When he went closer to look at what he had painted, he noticed a dead dog floating in the water. He was a very young painter.

Amateur painters are like novice bird-watchers attempting a birdcall; they haven't listened long enough to speak the language.

Art is not an object hanging on a wall. It must be a vehicle for ideas, intuition, and emotion. Painting as a language is timeless because of the pleasure people take in not only looking at art but in making it. Watch a child paint. It's as natural as laughter.

Painters gravitate toward other painters from whom they feel they can copy, just as people look for others whose moral frameworks align with their lifestyles.

Painting is nothing like eating. You're not just putting paint on the surface like you put food in your mouth; you must be thoughtful as you act. Painting is exactly like eating.

It's useless to try to create a style deliberately. Style is the combination of your idiosyncrasies and your labor exerted over time.

An earthworm paints in the soil. A crab paints on the sand. Humans, too, should paint naturally.

Paintings are desire mitigated by apathy and ennui. Paintings liberate a scene, and the distortions create a reality. This painted reality parallels the lived one. But the painted world is safe, and for most people, comfort generally supersedes veracity.

Painting is a long thread. Follow it.

Here's the story of a great painter: When she painted, she was happy.

When possible, avoid value judgments like "good" and "bad." There is only "practiced" and "unpracticed." Or focus on harmony and discord.

You've maybe heard this before, but if the success of your peers diminishes your appreciation of your work, then your work is less than theirs.

Focus less on who influences your work. Instead, ask who frees up your hands to experiment and take risks.

What you give to painting will return to you tenfold. Give observation, gain insight. Give discipline, and you'll be provided rest. But don't expect a painting to love you back; only other humans can do that—and most don't even care about painting.

Humaneness is the heart of painting, refracted through the lens of color.

The problem with aging as a painter is that the pictures you would let pass when you were younger no longer live up to your more experienced standards. This makes working even harder. You do see more clearly, but this added insight can be constraining.

As we get older, life becomes more familiar, and time accelerates. This is one of the reasons art is so important; it triumphs in the unfamiliar and slows the drumbeat of time.

I've always made bright, colorful paintings in winter. It seems the eye hungers for what is denied. Conversely, look at the work of the fabulous desert painter Agnes Martin. The colors are so subtle, as if washed out by the sun.

If you're afraid or paranoid about other artists stealing your ideas, you're probably guilty of theft yourself.

You don't have to believe in God or nature. You don't even have to believe in yourself. Just art, just painting.

No one cares about your art as much as you do. Nor should they! Children are important, as are family and friends. Paintings are simply the phantoms of visual history. Past thoughts and aesthetics pleasantly haunting the present.

Painting is no hobby. It's a lovely disease.

A painter once said, "A good picture is equivalent to a good deed." Not at all! Not even close. It may feel that way because we equate beauty with morality. But a good deed serves others first and you second. A good painting serves you first and others second—if it serves anyone at all.

Expectation has no place in painting.

Learn to love what you despise, and the whole world will be yours to paint.

Most of the time, people just walk past paintings—they're like trees to a passing dog. I'm not saying people who don't appreciate art are stupid, but like dogs, they have better things to do.

Painters, dreams told to strangers are far less interesting than true stories with high stakes. As you work, think about how to increase the stakes, the conflict, the drama. You do this by taking risks.

One fundamental characteristic of great painting is the creation of movement in depicting objects, even those at rest. Movement is life in the face of death. The ocean horizon appears still. But up close, you'd drown in the waves.

I knew an artist who couldn't listen to music while painting. She said her heart beat too loudly.

Walls divide people. Paintings, however, are the holes in the walls.

Painting destroys the illusion of separateness—the notion that humans are separate from trees, the ocean, rain, rocks, or any object. The canvas and personality unite. The breath leaves. The canvas stays.

Morning and mourning are homophones. When someone dies, something new begins. In painting, both words apply. Similarly, with the word painting, the noun and the verb are the same (anthimeria). But painting, like us, is more a verb than a noun.

These words, all of them, are tools of advice for no one but me. I'm sharing them because I believe some of the ideas may be useful to other painters. The truth is that we are all children, able to learn but unable to know, trapped in dying skins.

Painting is like penjing (bonsai in Japan). It is the whole world made small, cultivated over a lifetime.

Describing a painting is like trying to grab a fistful of the rain; the water just slips through your fingers.

If "speech is the image of actions," then painting is the image of action without speech.

Words used to frame painting—didactics—should not be necessary. A painting has to stand on its own, impossibly defying the biases of the present culture.

Critics are bees. They threaten but can do no actual harm unless they attack in great numbers.

Many painters fear not being recognized. We should change that. What we should fear is not painting. Or even better, nothing at all.

Painting survives, like a cockroach, because it is easy to hold, easy to hang, easy to transport, easy to store, easy to match to the decor, easy to look at, easy to love, and easy to do.

Contemporary painters are necessary because painting as an art form refuses to remain still. New blood pumps life into painting; young artists will forever wish to impose their egos on the medium.

To put it plainly, painting is not a secret code for mythical geniuses but rather a language available to anyone who wishes to lift a brush. The best part is, it doesn't even matter what you say.

To criticize painting is to defend its greatest iterations.

Most actions by human beings, especially in capitalist systems, entail pursuing ways to feel superior to their neighbor. Religion attempts to teach people that they are dust. Painting resides somewhere in between.

Humans have an insatiable need—to eat, procreate, and establish themselves as individuals. Religion provides an antidote by encouraging the reverse of the hunger: The doctrine emphasizes giving instead of taking. Great painting balances both. It fulfills the hunger of the creator but gifts something resonant to the world.

Art is a broad spectrum of languages with no applicable rules. Painters must develop their own identifiable grammar.

Colors, shapes, and text can be used interchangeably. Painting is language weighted toward aesthetics.

If there's one thing I know for sure, painting is a language open to anyone, like learning Spanish or practicing chi gong. There are those who are exceptional at these things, but this shouldn't discourage anyone. For too long, painting has been denied to the people because those versed in power (institutional aesthetics) deemed it theirs.

In painting, as in everything, follow the "natural course." If you're hungry, eat. Thirsty, drink. Paint when the urge is there. Paint, also, when it is not.

Painters must allow their minds and, more importantly, their eyes time to fast—to rest during waking hours. This heightens perception.

The best artists deftly camouflage their influences.

If you are a painter waiting to be discovered, you'll be waiting a long time. Most likely, you're not as great as you think, your work not as compelling as you imagine, and your life more boring than you can fathom. WONDERFUL! Painting doesn't care. It doesn't care about recognition as you do. Like a gene or a meme, it only wants to be carried on, to be practiced.

Painting's paradox: The language attracts introverts yet needs a community to thrive.

Even after you paint everything outside, and your guts as well, there's always more to paint. But I do understand why some painters might quit after many years. The faith fades. Without it, all that's left is self-importance. And there's nothing worse than an old, ugly narcissist.

The greatest painters are the greatest teachers, not through their words but through their works. Museums are schools of past thoughts.

The awakening of painting will occur when painters realize they must preserve the language for themselves, the speakers.

What is painting? Some say it is a means to reveal the transcendent voice of those with unmatched perceptive abilities. But this isn't so. It is a language for anyone. Painting, when practiced, helps develop one's perceptive abilities. Anyone can learn this.

As a banner to unify the people, a shared global language, painting may never compete with religion for the hearts of human beings. Still, there is a great deal of potential to unify those who, for so long, were left voiceless.

When it comes to the dialectic between individualism and collectivism, painting can be woven between these two ideas, uniting them. Though painters are usually individuals, painting is a global, historical, collective language.

Painting doesn't care what we do to it. We can criticize it, abolish it, outlaw it, encourage it, burn it, and store the results in musty basements. Painting is an action, like the wind—we can harness painting and saddle it with our dreams, but it remains indifferent to it all.

Maybe my best friends are all dead—past poets and painters who seem to know me better than I know myself.

You will find no truth in painting, only passing phases of imperfect understanding.

Sometimes, when in a quiet place, the absence of sound creates a vacuum, especially in old ears like mine. Sometimes, one of the ears may begin to ring. There's a tone like a bell inside the ear. The ear creates the tone. If that isn't painting, then I don't understand a thing about the world.

For most painters, it helps to unburden yourselves from the tyranny of history. Begin anew. The Language calls.

To paint faces, flowers, mountains, and winged things—who would ever want to die?

Paint and be done with it. "Eat the peach and toss away the stone."

Acknowledgments

When asked if they wished to thank anyone in an acknowledgments section for this book, The Painter responded with these four words: family, friends, teachers, cats.

About the Publisher

LOCATION was founded in 2010 as an artist-run, independent publisher dedicated to collaborative artist projects. Location books have been acquired by major museum libraries across the United States, including the Museum of Modern Art, the Whitney Museum of American Art, SFMOMA, the Minneapolis Institute of Art, and the Walker Art Center.

The second iteration of the project, LOCATION-BKS, began in 2024 with a mission to publish mass-market paperbacks by artists, allowing artists to reach a larger audience by utilizing a broad distribution network. LOCATION-BKS is committed to artists and to the innovative ideas that address the issues and aesthetics of our time.

Additional Reading

Barthes, Roland. Image—Music—Text. Translated by Stephen Heath. Hill and Wang, 1977.

Clark, T. J. The Painting of Modern Life: Paris in the Art of Manet and His Followers. Princeton University Press, 1985.

Gombrich, E. H. The Story of Art. 16th ed. Phaidon Press, 1995.

Henri, Robert. The Art Spirit. Basic Books, 2007.

Kandinsky, Wassily. Concerning the Spiritual in Art. Dover Publications, 1977.

Kimmelman, Michael. "Walk up. Wash Face. Do Routine. Now Paint." New York Times, May 8, 2005.

Laozi. Tao Te Ching. Translated by Stephen Mitchell. Harper Perennial, 1988.

Martin, Rebecca. Bouguereau: His Life and Works. Yale University Press, 2019.

Nochlin, Linda. The Politics of Vision: Essays on Nineteenth-Century Art and Society. Harper & Row, 1989.

Okakura, Kakuzō. The Book of Tea. Kodansha International, 2000.

Panofsky, Erwin. Meaning in the Visual Arts. Doubleday, 1955.

Princenthal, Nancy. Agnes Martin: Her Life and Art. Thames & Hudson, 2015.

Rilke, Rainer Maria. Duino Elegies. Trans. Charles L. C. Minor. The Four Seas Company, 1924.

Setiya, Kieran. Midlife: A Philosophical Guide. Princeton University Press, 2017.

Shunryu, Suzuki. Zen Mind, Beginner's Mind. Shambhala, 2011.

Sullivan, Michael. The Arts of China. 6th ed. University of California Press, 2008.

Tanizaki, Junichiro. In Praise of Shadows. Grove Press, 1977.

Van Gogh, Vincent. The Letters of a Post-Impressionist: Being the Familiar Correspondence of Vincent van Gogh. Translated by Anthony M. Ludovici. Houghton Mifflin Company, 1913.

Wittgenstein, Ludwig. Remarks on Colour. Edited by G. E. M. Anscombe. Translated by Linda L. McAlister and Margarete Schättle. Blackwell, 1977.

Zhuangzi. The Inner Chapters. Translated by Burton Watson. Columbia University Press, 2003.

L